Strategic Stability
in the Second Nuclear Age

COUNCIL *on*
FOREIGN
RELATIONS

Council Special Report No. 71
November 2014

Gregory D. Koblentz

Strategic Stability
in the Second Nuclear Age

Contents

Foreword

For much of the second half of the 20th century, the world lived with the very real specter of nuclear annihilation. The United States and the Soviet Union between them held some 60,000 nuclear weapons at the peak of the Cold War, more than enough to destroy each other several times over. Notwithstanding a few close calls, reason and caution increasingly gained the upper hand, and the United States and the Soviet Union reached accords and understandings that improved the transparency and stability of their arsenals.

Since the end of the Cold War, the nuclear picture has become more complex. To be sure, U.S. and Soviet inventories have come down significantly. But China, long a member of the nuclear club, is now a rising major power, with global interests that cast its nuclear arsenal in a new light. India and Pakistan both possess growing nuclear arsenals. Stockpiles in Europe are shrinking but are still meaningful. Israel, too, possesses a considerable number of nuclear weapons and delivery vehicles, although for its own reasons refuses to confirm this status. North Korea has a small inventory but its erratic behavior makes it more of a concern than the numbers alone would suggest. As Gregory Koblentz writes in this Council Special Report, this second nuclear age—one of more nuclear states connected in myriad ways—will pose more and different challenges to policymakers than was the case during the Cold War.

Koblentz highlights a number of challenges to strategic stability posed by this new era. The first challenge is that the "security dilemma" of the Cold War, in which actions taken by one state to secure itself made the other feel less secure, has given way to the "security trilemma": actions taken by one state to protect itself from a second make a third feel insecure. As states see and respond to the actions and perceived intentions of others, this dynamic could ripple through all the world's nuclear powers, which are connected by different but intersecting deterrence relationships. Technology, too, has the potential to threaten global strategic stability. As conventional weapons become stronger and more accurate, they can threaten even well-protected nuclear stockpiles. And cyberattacks can confuse or overwhelm early warning or communications systems, increasing vulnerability to a first strike. Instability in South Asia is the third risk Koblentz highlights. India and Pakistan both possess sizeable stockpiles with uncertain command and control. There is as well the potential for increased rivalry between China and India.

The United States has a clear interest in establishing a rigorous framework for strategic stability in the years ahead, Koblentz writes, and Washington should work to influence rules for this new age before a less amenable order crystallizes in place. Koblentz makes a number of recommendations. He calls for a long-term negotiating effort by the United States with the other six recognized nuclear states (China, France, India, Pakistan, Russia, and the United Kingdom) to address specific sources of instability, including missile defense, antisatellite weapons, and conventional counterforce systems. He also suggests initiating discussions on cybersecurity in the nuclear realm, with the goal of insulating nuclear systems from cyberattack. To improve the prospects for stability in South Asia, he recommends encouraging official and Track II dialogues among China, India, and Pakistan on nuclear issues, and building scientific and diplomatic capacity in India and Pakistan to enable discussions on these subjects. None of these recommendations, he cautions, should be seen as a replacement for bilateral strategic arms reductions, nor should they be seen as a replacement for the regional nuclear negotiations regarding Iran (designed to prevent it from becoming a state with nuclear weapons) and North Korea (designed in this case to persuade it to rid itself of its nuclear weapons). Rather, the goal of these seven-country talks is to shape long-term strategic stability among recognized nuclear states.

Strategic Stability in the Second Nuclear Age offers important insights into the state of nuclear stability in the post–Cold War era. It provides valuable analysis of the technical and political threats to that stability, and makes realistic recommendations for how to address them. As is the case with much else in the post–Cold War world, the task of maintaining nuclear stability promises to be even more difficult than it was in the previous era.

Richard N. Haass
President
Council on Foreign Relations
November 2014

Acknowledgments

I would like to express my gratitude to the many people who made this report possible. To begin, thank you to CFR President Richard N. Haass and Director of Studies James M. Lindsay for providing me the opportunity to author this report, and for their insightful feedback along the way.

The report's advisory committee was an invaluable resource and made the report better at every stage. In particular, I am grateful to advisory committee members who went above and beyond the call of duty—namely, James Acton, Craig G. Dunkerley, Michael A. Levi, and Micah Zenko. I owe a huge debt of gratitude to Linton F. Brooks and Steven K. Pifer, who served as the chairs of the advisory committee. I would also like to thank Martin Malin and Steven Miller at the Belfer Center for Science and International Affairs at the Harvard Kennedy School, who organized a helpful roundtable for me to discuss my early thinking on this issue. The report also benefited from interviews with numerous experts inside and outside of the government.

I am especially grateful for the excellent research assistance provided by Brian Mazanec and useful feedback from Margaret Midyette. I am also grateful for the logistical and research support of CFR Research Associate Jesse Sloman. I appreciate the contributions of the David Rockefeller Studies Program staff, particularly Amy Baker and Rachael Kauss, and Patricia Dorff in Publications in shepherding the report.

This work was made possible by a generous grant from the John D. and Catherine T. MacArthur Foundation. The statements made and views expressed herein are solely my own.

Gregory D. Koblentz

Council Special Report

Introduction

During the Cold War, the likelihood that nuclear weapons would be used deliberately, by accident, or in an unauthorized way was determined overwhelmingly by the actions of the United States and Soviet Union. Since the end of the Cold War, the locus of great power rivalry has shifted from Europe to Asia and new nuclear powers have emerged in that region, ushering in the second nuclear age.[1] Whereas the first nuclear age was shaped by the superpowers' nuclear arms race and global ideological competition, the second nuclear age is defined by the multiplicity of nuclear powers linked together by varying levels of cooperation and conflict. Although the United States and Soviet Union, and then Russia, eventually developed robust mechanisms for maintaining strategic stability, no such system exists to include the other nuclear-armed states.

Strategic stability in the second nuclear age faces three challenges. The first is the increasing complexity of deterrence relations among the nuclear weapon states. A central feature of the second nuclear age is that most nuclear weapon states face threats from two or more potential adversaries. This gives rise to a security trilemma where actions taken by a state to defend against another state have the effect of making a third state feel insecure.[2] Due to the trilemma, changes in one state's nuclear posture or policy can have a cascading effect on the other nuclear-armed states. The second challenge is the emergence of a suite of advanced nonnuclear military technologies, including missile defenses, antisatellite weapons, long-range precision strike systems, and cyber weapons, that have the potential to replicate, offset, or mitigate the strategic effects of nuclear weapons. The third challenge is found in South Asia, which is the region most at risk of a breakdown in strategic stability due to an explosive mixture of unresolved territorial disputes, cross-border terrorism, and growing nuclear arsenals. Furthermore, due to the security trilemma, the deterrence relationship between India and Pakistan is intertwined with that of China. This trilateral linkage increases the region's susceptibility to outside shocks and amplifies the risk that regional developments will have far-reaching effects. Each of these dynamics is worrisome on its own, but the combination of them could be particularly destabilizing.

The United States should, working in concert with the other nuclear weapon states, take a multipronged approach to strengthening strategic stability that addresses potential sources of instability in the near term and establishes processes that can contribute to multilateral nuclear arms control efforts over the longer term. The Obama administration should

- use a combination of transparency, confidence-building measures, and restraint to mitigate the risk that emerging technologies will endanger strategic stability by triggering arms races, threatening the survivability of nuclear forces, or undermining the integrity of early warning and nuclear command and control systems;
- deepen bilateral and multilateral dialogues with the other nuclear weapon states on strategic stability and build capacity within India and Pakistan to participate in such dialogues; and
- create a forum for the seven established nuclear weapon states to discuss further steps to strengthen strategic stability and reduce the risk of the deliberate, accidental, or unauthorized use of nuclear weapons.

The United States has more to lose from a breakdown in strategic stability—in the form of a nuclear conflict, crisis, accident, arms race, or act of terrorism—than any other country due to its position as a global leader, the interdependence of its economy, and the network of security commitments it has around the world. The highest U.S. priority is to maintain strategic stability with Russia and China, the two states with the capability and potential intent to launch a nuclear attack on the homeland. Though strategic stability is just one aspect of the United States' multifaceted relations with both countries, its enduring importance requires sustained high-level attention even during periods of international tension or in the face of unfavorable domestic politics. A failure of strategic stability that allowed nuclear weapons to fall into the hands of terrorists would also constitute a direct threat to U.S. national security. A breakdown in strategic stability among the other nuclear-armed states, such as China, India, and Pakistan, could also have catastrophic humanitarian, economic, and strategic consequences. The use of a nuclear weapon anywhere by anyone threatens U.S. national security by erasing the nuclear taboo. Due to its overwhelming conventional military capabilities, the United States benefits disproportionately from continuing the tradition of the nonuse of nuclear weapons.

Working with the other nuclear weapon states to strengthen strategic stability would serve U.S. national interests in a number of ways:

- Reduce the risk of nuclear weapons being used deliberately, by accident, or in an unauthorized manner.

- Improve crisis stability by increasing the confidence of nuclear weapon states that they possess secure and survivable nuclear forces and reducing the incentives for nuclear states to strike first during a crisis.

- Reduce the risk that nuclear modernization programs and the development of nonnuclear strategic technologies, such as missile defenses, antisatellite technologies, precision conventional strike weapons, and cyberwarfare, will trigger arms races that could threaten strategic stability.

- Promote transparency among nuclear-armed states on their nuclear doctrine, posture, and modernization plans. Such transparency is necessary for a substantive dialogue to build mutual understanding and pave the way for future reductions.

- Socialize the other nuclear-armed states into the arms control process, eventually including treaty negotiation, implementation, and verification.

- Create the opportunity to extend bilateral transparency and confidence-building measures already agreed to by the United States and Russia to other nuclear weapon states.

- Demonstrate the U.S. commitment to fulfilling its obligations under Article VI of the Treaty on the Non-Proliferation of Nuclear Weapons (NPT) and the Action Plan adopted by the 2010 NPT review conference.

- Create the conditions necessary for nuclear-armed states to participate in multilateral negotiations to limit and reduce their nuclear weapons in the future.

Strategic Landscape
of the Second Nuclear Age

There are seven established nuclear weapon states. China, France, Russia, the United Kingdom, and the United States are recognized as nuclear weapon states under the 1968 NPT. Since these states are also permanent members of the United Nations (UN) Security Council, they are commonly referred to as the P5. In 1998, India and Pakistan, neither of which has signed the NPT, conducted multiple nuclear tests, declared themselves to be nuclear weapon states, and publicly deployed nuclear-capable delivery systems. These seven states are estimated to possess 16,300 nuclear weapons (see Table 1).[3] Some 4,300 of these weapons are deployed on delivery systems or located at bases with operational launchers. Another 5,800 are stockpiled at various levels of readiness. The United States and

TABLE 1. STATUS OF NUCLEAR FORCES, 2014

Country	Operational Warheads	Reserve/ Nondeployed	Awaiting Dismantlement	Total Stockpile
Russia	1,800	2,700	3,500	8,000
United States	2,100	2,530	2,700	7,330
France	290	10	0	300
China	0	250	0	250
United Kingdom	160	65	0	225
Pakistan	0	~120	0	~120
India	0	~110	0	~110
TOTAL	4,350	5,785	6,200	16,335

Sources: Hans M. Kristensen and Robert S. Norris, "Global Nuclear Weapons Inventories, 1945-2013," *Bulletin of the Atomic Scientists* 69, no. 5, September/October 2013, pp. 75–81; Hans M. Kristensen and Robert S. Norris, "US Nuclear Forces, 2014," *Bulletin of the Atomic Scientists* 70, no. 1, January/February 2014, pp. 85–93; Hans M. Kristensen and Robert S. Norris, "Russian Nuclear Forces, 2014," *Bulletin of the Atomic Scientists* 70, no. 2, March/April 2014, pp. 75–85.

Russia possess an added 6,200 warheads that have been retired and are awaiting dismantlement.[4] Understanding the capabilities and motivations of these seven established nuclear weapon states is necessary to assess their role in maintaining or disrupting strategic stability.

Israel and North Korea are not included in this study. Although Israel possesses nuclear weapons, it has never officially acknowledged this fact. In addition, Israel is not in a deterrent relationship with any of the existing nuclear weapon states, limiting its influence on, and exposure to, variations in strategic stability among these states. North Korea has conducted three nuclear tests and claims to be a nuclear-armed state, however, "there is no conclusive evidence to suggest that North Korea has successfully produced a warhead or bomb capable of being delivered."[5] Since 2006, the UN Security Council has approved five resolutions demanding that North Korea abandon its nuclear weapon program and rejoin the NPT. Disarmament, rather than strategic stability, remains the appropriate framework for addressing the threats to international security posed by North Korea.

Multilateral efforts to address North Korea's and Israel's nuclear weapons programs have been severely hampered by the differing priorities of regional actors involved in the talks.[6] Since 2003, China, Japan, North Korea, Russia, South Korea, and the United States have participated in the Six Party Talks with the objective of denuclearizing the Korean peninsula. Since 2013, five rounds of talks have been held between Arab, Israeli, and other interested parties on holding a conference to establish a zone free of weapons of mass destruction in the Middle East. While neither set of efforts appear likely to bear fruit in the near future, resolving international concerns about North Korean and Israeli nuclear weapon programs will ultimately require regional solutions. For the time being, the United States and its partners should focus on revitalizing these initiatives instead of complicating issues further by linking them to broader efforts to strengthen strategic stability among the seven established nuclear powers.

THE SHRINKING GIANTS: UNITED STATES AND RUSSIA

Though the United States and Russia have dramatically reduced their nuclear stockpiles since the end of the Cold War, they still account for more than 90 percent of the world's nuclear weapons. The U.S.

nuclear stockpile consists of approximately 4,800 warheads, including 1,900 warheads that can be delivered by intercontinental ballistic missiles (ICBMs), submarine-launched ballistic missiles (SLBMs), and bombers, as well as 200 nonstrategic gravity bombs at bases in Europe (see Table 2).[7] Russia possesses approximately 4,300 nuclear warheads, of which roughly 1,600 strategic warheads are deployed on strategic missiles and at bomber bases (see Table 3).[8] Both countries keep a portion of their nuclear forces ready for launch at a moment's notice with the United States maintaining a higher proportion of its forces at this level than Russia.

Since the end of the Cold War, the United States and Russia have drawn down their nuclear arsenals while modernizing the triad of land-, air-, and sea-based strategic delivery systems. Under the New Strategic Arms Reduction Treaty (START), both countries will reduce their strategic nuclear arsenals to 1,550 deployed warheads on 700 deployed missiles and bombers by 2018. The United States is on the cusp of launching a major modernization program for every leg of its triad. Russia is in the middle of a large-scale procurement program to replace its Soviet-era missiles and submarines. Because the overall number of its deployed ICBMs will decrease, Russia is increasing the percentage of its force that can carry multiple independently targetable reentry vehicles (MIRVs).

The United States and Russia have different views on the utility of nuclear weapons. Nuclear weapons have played a declining role in U.S. national security since the end of the Cold War, but they remain a central element of national defense. Unique among the nuclear weapon states, the United States practices extended deterrence by providing the protection of its "nuclear umbrella" to thirty countries in Europe and Asia with which it has formal alliance commitments.[9] As a result, the United States views nuclear weapons as necessary for deterring not only nuclear attacks against the homeland by countries such as Russia and China, but also conventional and nuclear threats to its allies from those states and regional powers such as North Korea and Iran.[10]

Nuclear weapons have played an increasingly important role in Russia's national security strategy since the end of the Cold War. NATO enlargement and intervention in the Balkan conflicts during the 1990s highlighted the alliance's conventional military superiority and fed Russian suspicion that the alliance was not purely defensive. According

TABLE 2. U.S. NUCLEAR FORCES, 2014

Delivery System	Number Deployed	Year Deployed	Range (km)	Payload	Number of Warheads
Strategic Forces					1,902
Bombers					
B-52H	91	1961	16,000	ALCM: 5-150 KT	200
B-2A	20	1994	11,000	B-61, B-83	100
ICBM					
LGM-30G Minuteman III	450	1970	13,000	1 warhead x 300-355 KT	450
SSBNs/SLBMs					
Ohio-class SSBN	14	1981		24 Trident II D5 SLBMs	
UGM-133A Trident II D5 SLBM	288	1990	7,000	4 warheads x 100-455 KT	1,152
Nonstrategic Forces					200
B61 gravity bombs	NA	1979	Depends on delivery system	.3-170 KT	200
Total Deployed					2,102
Reserve					~2,530
Total Stockpile					4,632*
Awaiting Dismantlement					~2,700
Total Inventory					7,332

Source: Hans M. Kristensen and Robert S. Norris, "US Nuclear Forces, 2014," pp. 85–93.

*In May 2014, the United States announced that as of September 2013, its stockpile of strategic and nonstrategic active weapons (including operationally available and logistics spares) and inactive weapons (stored at a depot in a nonoperational status) was 4,804. Department of State, "Fact Sheet: Transparency in the U.S. Nuclear Weapons Stockpile," April 28, 2014.

TABLE 3. RUSSIAN NUCLEAR FORCES, 2014

Delivery System	Number Deployed	Year Deployed	Range (km)	Payload	Number of Warheads
Strategic Forces					
Bombers					
Tu-95MS6 (Bear-H6)	29	1984	6,500– 10,500	6 x ALCMs, bombs	174
Tu-95MS16 (Bear-H16)	30	1984	6,500– 10,500	16 x ALCMs, bombs	480
Tu-160 (Blackjack)	13	1987	10,500– 13,200	12 x ALCMs, bombs	156
ICBMs					
RS-20V (SS-18 Satan)	46	1988	11,000– 15,000	10 x 500/ 800 kt	460
RS-18 (SS-19 Stiletto)	30	1980	10,000	6 x 400 kt	180
RS-12M Topol (SS-25 Sickle)	117	1988	10,500	1 x 800 kt	117
RS-12M2 Topol-M (SS-27, silo)	60	1997	10,500	1 x 800 kt	60
RS-12M1 Topol-M (SS-27)	18	2006	10,500	1 x 800 kt	18
RS-24 Yars, mobile (SS-27 Mod 2)	33	2010	10,500	4 x 100 kt	132
RS-24 Yars, silo (SS-27 Mod 2)	—	2014	10,500	4 x 100 kt	—
RS-26 Yars-M/ Rubezh	—	2015	5,500+	?	—
Sarmat	—	(2018– 2020)	5,500+	?	—
SLBMs					
RSM-50 Volna (SS-N-18 M1 Stingray)	48	1978	6,500	3 x 50 kt	144
RSM-54 Sineva (SS-N-23 Skiff)	96	2007	9,000	4 x 100 kt	384
RSM-56 Bulava (SS-NX-32)	32	2014	8,050	6 x 100 kt	192

Delivery System	Number Deployed	Year Deployed	Range (km)	Payload	Number of Warheads
Nonstrategic Forces					
Air Defense, Missile Defense, and Coastal Defense					
53T6 (SH-08, Gazelle)	68	1986	30	1 x 10 kt	68
S-300 (SA-10/ 12/20)	1,000	1980/2007	—	1 x low kt	~340
SSC-1B (Sepal)	34	1973	500	1 x 350	~17
Tactical Aircraft					
Tu-22M3 (Backfire-C)	150	1974	—	3 x ASM, bombs	~450
Su-24M/M2 (Fencer-D)	260	1974	—	2 x bombs	~260
Su-34 (Fullback)	20	2006	—	2 x bombs	~20
Land-Based Short-Range Ballistic Missiles					
OTR-21 Tochka (SS-21 Scarab)	140	1981	120	1 x 10 kt	~140
Iskander-M (SS-26 Stone)	30	2005	300	1 x 10 kt	~30
Ground-Launched Cruise Missile					
Iskander-K/R-500	?	2014	500+	?	?
Naval					
SLCM, ASW, SAM, depth charges, torpedoes	—	—	—	—	~700
Total Strategic Stockpile					2,499
Total Nonstrategic Stockpile					~2,025
Total Stockpile					~4,525
Awaiting Dismantlement					3,500
Total Inventory					~8,025

Sources: Stockholm International Peace Research Institute (SIPRI), *SIPRI Yearbook 2013: Armaments, Disarmament and International Security* (Oxford: Oxford University Press, 2013), pp. 294–95; Hans M. Kristensen and Robert S. Norris, "Russian Nuclear Forces, 2014," pp. 75–85; Hans M. Kristensen, "Russia Declared In Violation of INF Treaty: New Cruise Missile May Be Deploying," Federation of American Scientists, July 30, 2014.

to Russia's 2010 military doctrine, "Russia reserves the right to use nuclear weapons in response to the use of nuclear and other weapons of mass destruction against Russia and/or its allies and in case of aggression against the Russian Federation involving conventional weapons when the very existence of the State is under threat."[11] Although the United States and NATO remain the primary focus of Russian nuclear planning, China's territorial claims and large conventional forces are also of concern, albeit one that is not openly discussed.[12]

THE SECOND-TIER NUCLEAR POWERS

Since the end of the Cold War, the United Kingdom and France have unilaterally reduced the number, types, and readiness levels of their nuclear weapons. The United Kingdom currently possesses 225 nuclear weapons that can be deployed on four Vanguard-class fleet ballistic missile submarines, or SSBNs (see Table 4). It plans on reducing its overall stockpile to 180 warheads by the mid-2020s, which would give it the smallest nuclear stockpile among the original five nuclear weapon states. In 2016, the United Kingdom will decide on how to replace its Vanguard submarines, which are due to be retired in the late 2020s.[13] France has declared that it possesses three hundred warheads that can be launched from aircraft and from four Triomphant-class SSBNs (see Table 5).[14] Both France and the United Kingdom have announced that they do not maintain their nuclear weapons at a high-alert level.[15]

The threat posed by Russian conventional and nuclear forces remains central to both states' nuclear planning, although their declaratory doctrines are couched in much broader terms. The United Kingdom has declared that "we would only consider using our nuclear weapons in extreme circumstances of self-defence, including the defence of our NATO Allies, and we remain deliberately ambiguous about precisely when, how and at what scale we would contemplate their use."[16] According to the latest French Defense White Paper, "Nuclear deterrence protects France from any State-led aggression against its vital interests, of whatever origin and in whatever form. It rules out any threat of blackmail that might paralyse its freedom of decision and action."[17]

TABLE 4. BRITISH NUCLEAR FORCES, 2013

Delivery System	Number Deployed	Year Deployed	Range (km)	Payload	Number of Warheads
SSBNs					
Vanguard	4	1994	NA	16 x Trident II D5 SLBMs	
SLBMs					
Trident II D5	48	1994	>7,400	1-3 x 100 kt	225
Total Inventory					225

Source: SIPRI, *SIPRI Yearbook 2013,* p. 301.

TABLE 5. FRENCH NUCLEAR FORCES, 2013

Delivery System	Number Deployed	Year Deployed	Range (km)	Payload	Number of Warheads
Bombers					
Mirage 2000N	~20	1988	2,750	1 x Air-Sol Moyenne Portee Amélioré (ASMPA): up to 300 kt	~20
Rafale F3	~30	2010–2011	2,000	1 x ASPMA: up to 300 kt	~30
SSBN/SLBMs					
Triomphant	4	1997	NA	16 SLBMs	
M45	32	1996	6,000	4–6 x 100 kt	160
M51.1	16	2010–2011	6,000	4–6 x 100 kt	80
M51.2	—	2015	6,000	4–6 x 150 kt	—
Total Assigned Stockpile					~290
Reserve					~10
Total Inventory					300

Source: SIPRI, *SIPRI Yearbook 2013,* p. 304.

THE RISING NUCLEAR POWERS: CHINA, PAKISTAN, AND INDIA

Though nuclear arsenals are shrinking in the rest of the world, Asia is witnessing a nuclear buildup. Unlike the remaining P5 countries, China is increasing and diversifying its nuclear arsenal. Pakistan and India have been involved in a nuclear and missile arms race since 1998 that shows no signs of abating. Although both states claim to seek only a credible minimum deterrent, regional dynamics have driven them to pursue a range of nuclear and missile capabilities. All three states shroud their nuclear and missile programs in intense secrecy, which complicates the ability of outside observers to accurately gauge their intentions and capabilities.

CHINA

China is estimated to have 250 nuclear weapons for delivery by a mix of medium-, intermediate-, and intercontinental-range ballistic missiles, SSBNs (none of which are believed to have conducted operational patrols yet), and bombers (see Table 6). China claims that the fundamental goal of its nuclear weapons is "to deter other countries from using or threatening to use nuclear weapons against China."[18] Since 1964, China has adopted a no-first-use (NFU) doctrine and has promised not to threaten or use nuclear weapons against nonnuclear weapon states.

China has gradually modernized its nuclear forces since the end of the Cold War in keeping with its stated goal of deploying "lean and effective" nuclear forces capable of retaliating against a first strike.[19] The introduction of road-mobile ICBMs and a new generation of SSBNs armed with new SLBMs should significantly improve the survivability of China's strategic nuclear forces.[20] China maintains its nuclear forces at a low level of operational readiness, storing warheads separately from delivery systems. China has the capability to deploy multiple warheads on its missiles but is not believed to have done so yet.[21]

PAKISTAN

Pakistan, which has the fastest growing nuclear weapon program in the world, is believed to have enough fissile material to produce between 110 and 120 nuclear warheads.[22] By 2020, Pakistan could have a fissile

TABLE 6. CHINESE NUCLEAR FORCES, 2013

Delivery System	Number Deployed	Year Deployed	Range (km)	Payload	Number of Warheads
Bombers					
H-6 (B-6)	~20	1965	3,100	1 x bomb or possibly cruise missile	~20
Attack	—	1972	—	1 x bomb	~20
Land-Based Missiles					
DF-3A (CSS-2)	~12	1971	3,100	1 x 3.3 Mt	~12
DF-4 (CSS-3)	~12	1980	5,500	1 x 3.3 Mt	~12
DF-5A (CSS-4)	20	1981	13,000	1 x 4–5 Mt	20
DF-15 (CSS-6)	~350	1990	600	1 x Unknown	Unknown
DF-21 (CSS-5)	~60	1991	2,100	1 x 200–300 kt	~60
DF-31 (CSS-10 Mod 1)~20		2006	>7,200	1 x 200–300 kt	~20
DF-31A (CSS-10 Mod 2)~20		2007	>11,200	1 x 200–300 kt	~20
Ground-Launched Cruise Missile					
DH-10 (CJ-10) 150–350		2007	>1,500	Unclear if nuclear	Unknown
SLBMs					
JL-1 (CSS-N-3)	~12	1986	>1,770	1 x 200–300 kt	~12
JL-2 (CSS-NX-14)	~36	~2013	>7,400	1 x 200–300 kt	~36
Total Inventory					~250

Source: SIPRI, *SIPRI Yearbook 2013*, p. 306.

material stockpile sufficient to produce more than two hundred nuclear weapons.[23] Pakistan has deployed or is developing eleven delivery systems for its nuclear warheads, including aircraft, ballistic missiles, and cruise missiles (see Table 7). Pakistan reportedly keeps its warheads stored separately from launchers.[24] Pakistan has not formally declared the conditions under which it would use nuclear weapons but has indicated that it seeks primarily to deter India from threatening its territorial integrity or the ability of its military to defend its territory.[25]

TABLE 7. PAKISTANI NUCLEAR DELIVERY SYSTEMS, 2013

Delivery System	Year Deployed (First Tested)	Range (km)	Payload (kg)	Status
Aircraft				
F-16A/B	1998	1,600	4,500	
Mirage V	1998	2,100	4,000	
Ballistic Missiles				
Abdali (Hatf-2)	(2012)	~180	200–400	Under development
Ghaznavi (Hatf-3)	2004	290	500	Fewer than 50 Hatf-1, 3, 4, & 9 launchers (combined)
Shaheen I (Hatf-4)	2003	650	750–1,000	Fewer than 50 Hatf-1, 3, 4, & 9 launchers (combined)
Ghauri (Hatf-5)	2003	>1,200	700–1,000	Fewer than 50 launchers
Shaheen II (Hatf-6)	2011	2,500	~1,000	Unknown number of launchers
Nasr (Hatf-9)	2013	~60	Unknown	Fewer than 50 Hatf-1, 3, 4, & 9 launchers (combined)
Cruise Missiles				
Babur (Hatf-7)	(2005)	600	400–500	Under development; ground launched
Ra'ad (Hatf-8)	(2007)	350	Unknown	Under development; air launched

Sources: SIPRI, *SIPRI Yearbook 2013,* pp. 284, 318, 320; Hans M. Kristensen and Robert S. Norris, "Pakistan's Nuclear Forces 2011," *Bulletin of the Atomic Scientists* 67, no. 4, July/August 2011, pp. 91–99; National Air and Space Intelligence Center, "Ballistic and Cruise Missile Threat," 2013.

TABLE 8. INDIAN NUCLEAR DELIVERY SYSTEMS, 2013

Delivery System	Year Deployed (First Tested)	Range (km)	Payload (kg)	Status
Bombers				
Mirage 2000H	1985	1,850	6,300	
Land-Based Ballistic Missiles				
Prithvi I/II	1994	150/ 350	800/ 500	Fewer than 75 Prithvi and Agni I launchers (combined)
Agni I	2004	~700	1,000	Fewer than 75 Prithvi and Agni I launchers (combined)
Agni II	2004	2,000	1,000	Fewer than 10 launchers
Agni III	(2006)	~3,000	1,500	Under development
Agni IV	(2011)	~4,000	1,000	Under development
Agni V	(2012)	>5,000	~1,000	Under development
Ship-Launched Ballistic Missiles				
Dhanush	?	350	500	Induction under way but probably not operational
SSBNs				
INS Arihant	[2015]	NA	4 SLBMs	Undergoing sea trials
SLBMs				
K-15/B-05	(2010)	700	500– 600	Under development; to be deployed on Arihant
K-4	(2014)	3,000	?	Under development

Sources: SIPRI, *SIPRI Yearbook 2013*, pp. 284, 312; Hans M. Kristensen and Robert S. Norris, "Indian Nuclear Forces 2012," *Bulletin of the Atomic Scientists* 68, no. 4, July/August 2014, p. 100; National Air and Space Intelligence Center, "Ballistic and Cruise Missile Threat," 2013; Yogesh Joshi and Frank O'Donnell, "India's Submarine Deterrent and Asian Nuclear Proliferation," *Washington Quarterly* 56, no. 4, August/ September 2014, pp. 157–74.

While Pakistan is focused predominantly on the threat posed by India, it is reportedly also concerned by the potential for the United States to launch a military operation to seize or disarm Pakistani nuclear weapons. This concern is based in part on reported contingency planning by the U.S. military to prevent Pakistani nuclear weapons from falling into the hands of terrorists. Pakistan's sensitivity to such a disarming operation was heightened by the 2011 Abbottabad raid that killed Osama bin Laden because it revealed Pakistani vulnerabilities and highlighted the willingness of the United States to take unilateral military action on Pakistani soil.[26] Pakistani officials, however, deny that these concerns affect Pakistan's nuclear force posture or plans.[27]

INDIA

India is estimated to possess enough fissile material for between 90 and 110 nuclear weapons and is expanding its fissile material production capacity. India currently fields nuclear-capable aircraft and ballistic missiles and is developing longer-range ballistic missiles, including a version capable of carrying MIRVs; a ballistic missile that can be fired from a surface ship; ground-, air-, and sea-launched cruise missiles; and a nuclear-powered submarine capable of launching SLBMs (see Table 8). Traditionally, India has kept its warheads disassembled and separate from launchers but it may keep a small number of systems at a higher level of readiness.[28]

Since its first nuclear test in 1974, India has publicly adhered to a no-first-use policy. According to its 2003 nuclear doctrine, India seeks a "credible minimum deterrent" to deter nuclear attacks on its territory and armed forces and vows that its response to a first strike would be "massive and designed to inflict unacceptable damage."[29] In addition, this doctrine qualified India's NFU policy to allow for the use of nuclear weapons in response to a major chemical or biological attack. Prime Minister Narendra Modi, who entered office in May 2014, has pledged to review India's nuclear doctrine.[30]

Challenges to Strategic Stability

Strategic stability is a slippery concept that can be defined in many ways.[31] In their classic 1961 book *Strategy and Arms Control*, Nobel Prize–winning economist Thomas Schelling and Morton Halperin defined strategic stability as a situation where the risks of war are low because neither side has an incentive to strike first and this calculation is "reasonably secure against shocks, alarms and perturbations."[32] The essence of strategic stability is limiting the incentives for states to launch a first strike while at the same time increasing their confidence that they will be able to launch a second. Under those conditions, states will face less pressure during a crisis to escalate a conflict, to respond quickly to incomplete information, or to deploy their forces in a way that might unnecessarily provoke the other side. In effect, strategic stability refers to the likelihood that nuclear weapons will be used intentionally, accidently, inadvertently, or without authorization. Schelling and Halperin identified a range of conditions and behaviors that could endanger strategic stability which are still relevant today: strategic weapons that are vulnerable to a first strike, weapons that are accident prone, early warning systems with high false alarm rates, unreliable command and control systems, strategic weapons susceptible to obsolescence due to technical breakthroughs, force postures that place a premium on rapid decision-making, the delegation of launch authority that complicates the control of weapons during a crisis or war, and weapons that rely on surprise for their effectiveness.

Three current trends have the potential to disrupt strategic stability: the emergence of security trilemmas among the nuclear weapon states, the development of nonnuclear technologies with potentially strategic effects, and the unstable balance between India and Pakistan in South Asia. Each of these dynamics is worrisome on their own, but the combination of them could be particularly destabilizing. If these three trends are not handled carefully, they could not only endanger strategic stability in the near term but also set back the prospects for multilateral arms control in the future.

THE SECURITY TRILEMMA

The second nuclear age has ushered in a new geometry of deterrence. During the Cold War, the United States and Soviet Union were faced with a security dilemma: efforts by one state to increase its security were invariably viewed as a threat by the other side. When the threatened state responded with its own measure, it only increased the insecurity of the other state. This dynamic helps explain the nuclear arms race between the superpowers and their intense competition for allies and influence around the world.

In the second nuclear age, most nuclear weapon states face security threats from more than one source. This development creates what Linton Brooks and Mira Rapp-Hooper term the security trilemma: actions taken by one state to defend against another state have the effect of making a third state feel insecure.[33] The overlapping bilateral deterrence relationships among nuclear states creates the potential for changes in the capabilities or intentions of one state to have a cascading effect on the rest of the nuclear weapon states (see Figure 1).

With the security trilemma acting as a transmission belt, developments that might have mattered only at a bilateral level now have the

FIGURE 1. NUCLEAR WEAPON STATE DETERRENT RELATIONSHIPS[34]

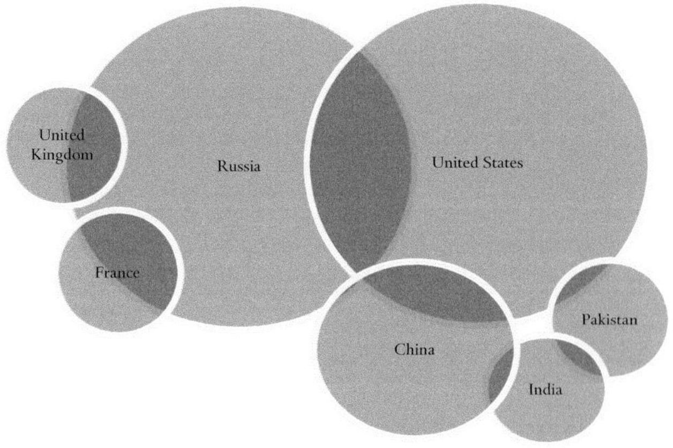

potential to have much wider strategic consequences. With the exception of the United Kingdom and France, who each view only one state (Russia) as posing an existential threat, the other nuclear weapon states face multiple nuclear and conventional threats to their national security. This dynamic is particularly strong in Asia. For example, the United States claims that its national missile defense system and development of long-range precision strike capabilities are motivated by the threats posed by countries such as Iran and North Korea. China and Russia, however, view these systems as potential threats to the survivability of their strategic nuclear forces. China's responses to these developments, such as the modernization of its nuclear forces and development of anti-satellite (ASAT) and missile defense capabilities, has triggered a reaction from India, which causes grave concern in Pakistan. In turn, the 2005 U.S.-Indian Civil Nuclear Agreement triggered a new round of nuclear technology sales by China to Pakistan.[35]

TECHNOLOGICAL DEVELOPMENTS

Nuclear weapons may have been the "absolute weapon" during the Cold War, but other technologies are emerging that can replicate, offset, or mitigate the strategic effects of those weapons. A suite of non-nuclear technologies, including missile defense, antisatellite weapons, long-range precision strike systems, and cyber weapons, have emerged that have the potential to undermine strategic stability. These technologies present challenges to strategic stability in the near term (missile defense), medium term (conventional counterforce and antisatellite weapons), and long term (cyber weapons). Even though some of these capabilities are years from deployment and others are deployed in only a limited fashion, it is natural for military planners to conduct worst-case assessments in anticipation of future technological advances or expanded deployments. This dynamic reinforces the action-reaction cycle and "zero-sum" mentality that feeds the security trilemma.

MISSILE DEFENSE

Missile defenses can reduce strategic stability between two comparably armed nuclear states in two ways. Missile defenses can undermine deterrence stability by limiting the ability of a state to inflict unacceptable damage against an attacker after suffering a first strike. By reducing a state's confidence in its ability to carry out a devastating retaliatory strike after suffering a first strike, missile defenses provide incentives for that state to strike first if it believes it is about to be attacked, or to adopt a "launch under attack" posture to maximize the number of missiles that can survive a first strike and attempt to penetrate the attacker's missile defenses. Missile defense, however, is an incredibly complex and expensive undertaking. States can equip their missiles with countermeasures or MIRVs to overwhelm the defender, as well as build more missiles. Thus, the introduction of nation-wide missile defenses risks sparking an arms race, the second danger to strategic stability. By banning the deployment of national missile defenses, the 1972 Anti-Ballistic Missile (ABM) Treaty removed this threat to strategic stability between the superpowers.

In 2002, the United States withdrew from the ABM Treaty and began deploying a national missile defense system to defend against long-range missiles under development by North Korea. By 2014, the system comprised thirty interceptors in Alaska and California with another fourteen planned by 2017.[36] In 2009, President Obama announced the European Phased Adaptive Approach (EPAA) plan to defend against short-, medium-, and intermediate-range missiles launched by Iran. U.S. Navy ships now provide the initial missile defense capability with two land-based sites set to become operational by 2018.[37] The United States also deploys a mix of sea- and land-based missile defense systems in East Asia designed to target short- to intermediate-range missiles.[38]

The United States has stressed that its development and deployment of missile defenses are designed to counter threats from regional actors such as Iran and North Korea and are not capable of threatening, or intended to threaten, the nuclear forces of Russia or China.[39] While Russian and Chinese officials acknowledge the limited nature of current U.S. missile defense systems, they remain concerned that the United States is creating a global architecture of launch facilities, sensors, and command and control networks into which increasingly capable interceptors can be deployed over time. Given their smaller ICBM force and lack of MIRVs, China has been particularly vocal about the threat that a multilayered missile defense system poses to its retaliatory capacity.[40]

Missile defense also has the potential to upset strategic stability in Asia. India has been pursuing a missile defense capability since the early

1990s, motivated primarily by a desire to counter Pakistan's ballistic missiles.[41] Although India's indigenous research and foreign procurement efforts have so far not yielded a meaningful capability, its missile defense efforts spurred Pakistan's development of nuclear-capable cruise missiles, introducing a new element of instability into the South Asian nuclear balance.[42]

China is also developing missile defense technologies, having conducted four intercept tests in the last three years.[43] It is unclear whether the purpose of the tests is to better understand the capabilities and limitations of missile defense technology, as a cover for antisatellite testing, or as part of a program to deploy an operational missile defense system.[44] Regardless of the motivation, China's tests have "upped the ante" in the region and are likely to trigger an Indian response which will spark a Pakistani reaction.[45] While operational missile defense capabilities in China and South Asia remain years away, the anticipated introduction of such systems may drive all three states to pursue qualitative and quantitative improvements to their nuclear forces in the near term.

ANTISATELLITE

Antisatellite weapons can reduce strategic stability in two ways.[46] First, ASAT weapons can be used to destroy an adversary's early-warning satellites intended to detect an incoming ballistic missile attack. Second, ASAT weapons could undermine strategic stability by threatening space-based nuclear command and control systems, making a "decapitating" attack more viable. ASAT capabilities could therefore heighten concerns regarding the prospect of an undetected first strike on nuclear forces as well as complicate a state's ability to control, limit, or terminate a conflict once it begins. At this time, only Russia and the United States use satellites for these purposes although China and India are developing increasingly sophisticated military satellite capabilities that may eventually include early warning and command and control functions.[47]

During the Cold War, the United States and Soviet Union developed limited ASAT capabilities but since neither side deployed them on a large scale, their effect on strategic stability was muted.[48] Russia has indicated a renewed interest in ASAT weapons but the operational status of any such weapons is unclear.[49] The United States does not have an official ASAT program, but its land- and sea-based midcourse missile defense systems are also capable of intercepting satellites. This latent capability was demonstrated in 2008 when the United States successfully shot down a defunct military satellite with a modified SM-3 missile fired from an Aegis cruiser.[50] China has tested a missile capable of intercepting satellites at least seven times since 2005. In 2007, the Chinese used a missile to destroy a defunct weather satellite, which generated a large amount of space debris and an international backlash against China.[51] In 2010, in response to China's tests, India announced that it was launching its own ASAT program.[52] This more complex multilateral development of ASAT capabilities poses a new risk to strategic stability.

CONVENTIONAL COUNTERFORCE

During the first nuclear age, uncertainty about the exact locations of targets, the hardness of vital targets such as ICBM silos and command and control bunkers, and the limited accuracy of delivery systems meant that nuclear weapons were the best, if not only, way to implement a counterforce strategy to destroy an adversary's nuclear weapons. The revolution in military affairs ushered in by precision-guided munitions, combined with the expansion of intelligence, surveillance, and reconnaissance capabilities, has given rise to conventional counterforce: the ability to use precision conventional weapons to destroy targets whose destruction once required nuclear weapons. The development of non-nuclear precision-guided weapons capable of destroying hardened and buried targets are viewed by the United States as a way to reduce its reliance on nuclear weapons for striking this class of targets and, if mounted on a long-range ballistic missile, to offer nonnuclear options for striking critical, time-sensitive targets.[53] Since 2001, the most high-profile effort to develop such a capability has been the Conventional Prompt Global Strike (CGPS) program.[54] The search for conventional alternatives to nuclear weapons, however, has created an asymmetry in favor of the United States that creates new risks to strategic stability and makes other states less willing to reduce their own reliance on nuclear weapons.

Conventional counterforce weapons present four risks to strategic stability.[55] First, a conventionally armed ICBM or SLBM would have the same flight profile, and perhaps the same flight path, as a nuclear-armed version, raising the prospect that another state would interpret the launch of such a weapon as a nuclear attack. A U.S. National Academy of Sciences report concluded that "the ambiguity between nuclear and conventional payloads can never be totally resolved."[56] The second risk is that these weapons would undermine deterrence stability by enabling an attacker to launch a first strike on an adversary's nuclear forces without using nuclear weapons. This capability would be particularly destabilizing if the attacker also possessed a missile defense system that could potentially intercept any missiles that survived the first strike. Third, using conventionally armed missiles against the conventional forces of a nuclear weapon state might be misinterpreted by that state as an attack aimed at its nuclear forces, which could lead to escalation. This risk is heightened for countries that use multiple variants of the same delivery system for nuclear and conventional missions and comingle nuclear and conventional delivery systems. Fourth, development of this new type of capability could spark an arms race driven by a desire to emulate the world's greatest military power, the allure of a new type of military technology, or the perceived need for a deterrent.

Russia and China have voiced strong concerns about the United States' development of what Russians call strategic conventional weapons for all of these reasons. The United States has addressed the risk of ambiguity by abandoning the concept for a conventionally armed SLBM and focusing on launch vehicles that use hypersonic glider reentry vehicles that have a different trajectory than nuclear-armed ballistic missiles.[57] The United States has attempted to address the second concern by emphasizing that CGPS is a "niche" capability, implying that only a small number would need to be acquired. Neither of these steps, however, has assuaged Russian and Chinese concerns. Moscow and Beijing hold deep-seated suspicions about the true purpose of these weapons, likely overestimate the pace and sophistication of U.S. research in this field, and fear that a limited capability could grow over time. As a result, there is evidence that China and Russia have joined the United States in a "hypersonic arms race."[58] Finally, although conventionally armed ballistic missiles have received most of the attention, Russia and China are also concerned about the growing capabilities of U.S. air-delivered precision-guided munitions and sea-launched cruise missiles to target their hardened and mobile nuclear forces.[59] Since these weapons have become integral to U.S. military operations, there is little prospect for restraining their deployment or usage.

CYBERWARFARE

The vulnerability of nuclear command and control systems to a so-called decapitation attack that prevents a nation's leadership from ordering a retaliatory strike has long been recognized as a threat to strategic stability.[60] A leadership that fears that it is about to suffer such an attack will be under tremendous pressure to launch its own attack first. Cyberwarfare presents a new potential threat to nuclear command and control systems.[61] The Stuxnet computer worm that sabotaged Iran's uranium enrichment program, Edward Snowden's revelations about the United States' offensive cyber capabilities, and allegations of Russian and Chinese cyber espionage against sensitive U.S. military and industrial computer systems have demonstrated the ability of government-sponsored hackers to penetrate the most secure computer networks in the world. In 2013, the U.S. Defense Science Board and the commander of U.S. Strategic Command expressed concern about the potential vulnerability of the U.S. nuclear command and control system to a sophisticated cyberattack.[62] Given the multiple levels of authorization needed to launch a nuclear attack, the possibility that a hacker could hijack control of U.S. nuclear forces to launch an attack is not credible. Indeed, the 1970s provenance of the Minuteman III, including command centers that upload instructions using floppy disks, provides some protection against cyberattacks.[63]

More realistic scenarios include the spoofing of early warning systems to create false alarms or to suppress the signs of an attack. In 1979 and 1980, the North American Aerospace Defense Command (NORAD) experienced a number of false alarms due to internal technical glitches.[64] In 2007, an Israeli airstrike against a reactor under construction in Syria was reportedly accompanied by a cyberattack that blinded Syria's formidable air defense system.[65] Another potential concern is virtual decapitation by disrupting communications between the national command authority and nuclear force commanders. In 2010, for example, a hardware glitch caused the Air Force to temporarily lose contact with fifty Minuteman III ICBMs, one-ninth of the nation's ICBM force.[66]

The use of cyber weapons against the command and control system of a state's nuclear arsenal qualifies as what Schelling and Halperin called mischief, an act that provides a temporary advantage but leaves both sides worse off if they both conduct it.[67] Impeding an adversary's ability to communicate with its forces and coordinate military action might have operational advantages, but disrupting nuclear command and control also creates a number of risks.[68] In an extreme case, if a country's leadership feared that its nuclear command and control system had been compromised and that it might lose the ability to use its nuclear weapons even in retaliation, it might decide to use the weapons preemptively. During the Cold War, the superpowers responded to the threat of decapitation by adopting a "launch-on-warning" posture, which relied on early warning of an attack, rapid decision-making, nuclear forces maintained at a high level of readiness, and the delegation of launch authority.[69] Given the novelty of cyber threats to nuclear command and control, it remains to be seen how states will respond to this emerging threat and what effect their countermeasures might have on strategic stability.

INSTABILITY IN SOUTH ASIA

India and Pakistan face more severe security challenges than those of the other nuclear weapon states due to their history of high-intensity and low-intensity conflicts, higher levels of domestic instability, geographic proximity, the dispute over Kashmir that has existential implications for both countries, and the history of cross-border terrorism. The next crisis between India and Pakistan could be sparked by a cross-border military incursion, a mass-casualty terrorist attack or a high-profile assassination. The growth of nuclear and missile capabilities on the subcontinent since 1998 has increased the risk that such a crisis could escalate in unforeseen and dangerous ways. The security trilemma increases the vulnerability of regional stability to disruptions by outside forces and increases the likelihood that a breakdown in strategic stability between India and Pakistan could threaten other nuclear weapon states.

   The size and composition of Pakistan's nuclear forces appear increasingly dictated by India's growing conventional military capabilities. In response to Pakistani military interventions such as the 1999 Kargil incursion and cross-border terrorism originating from Pakistan, the Indian Army has developed a new doctrine (initially called Cold Start but now known as "proactive strategy") of rapid, limited conventional military operations designed to remain below Pakistan's presumed nuclear threshold. To counter the potential for limited Indian intrusions, Pakistan has begun deploying tactical nuclear weapons, such as the Hatf IX short-range ballistic missile, under the rubric of "full-spectrum deterrence."[70] Since the conventional military imbalance between India and Pakistan is expected to grow thanks to India's larger economy and higher gross domestic product (GDP) growth rate, Pakistan's reliance on nuclear weapons to compensate for its conventional inferiority will likely be an enduring feature of the nuclear balance in South Asia.[71]

Potential changes in Pakistan's nuclear posture have direct implications for U.S. national security, which has placed a high priority on preventing terrorists from acquiring nuclear weapons. One of the most worrisome risks introduced by Pakistan's deployment of tactical nuclear weapons, especially acute during a crisis, is what Scott Sagan calls the "vulnerability/invulnerability paradox": measures that allow a state's nuclear forces to withstand a first strike, such as mating warheads to mobile missiles and dispersing them, also make them more vulnerable to theft or terrorist takeover.[72] The strong presence of domestic extremists and foreign jihadi groups in Pakistan, their demonstrated ability to penetrate the security of military facilities, and evidence that they have infiltrated the security services, magnify the risks that terrorists could breach Pakistan's nuclear security.[73]

Another worrisome development is that the Indian and Pakistani practice of storing their nuclear warheads separately from launchers, which has provided a strong barrier to nuclear escalation in the past, may be eroding. Pakistan's deployment of tactical nuclear weapons on short-range missiles and India's development of a sea-based deterrent may lead both states to loosen their highly centralized command and control practices.[74] Granting lower-ranking officers greater authority and capability to arm and launch nuclear weapons raises the risk of unauthorized actions during a crisis or inadvertent escalation during a conventional conflict by a local commander of a nuclear-armed unit who finds himself in a "use it or lose it" situation. The Indian and Pakistani practice of not clearly demarcating which of their aircraft and missiles are assigned conventional and nuclear missions further increases the risk of the latter scenario. The short flight times of ballistic missiles between India and Pakistan exacerbate these tensions by sharply reducing decision-making timelines for government officials during a crisis.

Indian and Pakistani nuclear and missile developments can not only have negative consequences for regional stability but can also influence the nuclear postures of other nuclear-armed states, especially China.[75] Since 1998, India has publicly justified many of its nuclear and missile initiatives based on the threat posed by China. India and China fought a brief border war in 1962 and have a number of potential flash points between them, including long stretches of their border that are disputed or not fully demarcated, China's claim on the Indian state of Arunachal Pradesh, India's support for Tibetan independence, and competition for control of the Himalayan headwaters.[76] In addition, India interprets China's support for Pakistan's nuclear and missile programs as evidence of China's hostile intent toward India. Given China's rise as a great power and its growing assertiveness over territorial disputes, there are some strategic sources of India's threat perception. Broader calculations about power and status, however, also appear to play a role. In short, India views China as a worthy adversary and peer competitor, but not Pakistan.

China does not view India in the same way, at least not yet. There is the potential, however, for Chinese threat perceptions to change as India's capability catches up to its rhetoric.[77] India's 2012 test of the intermediate range Agni-V ballistic missile marked the first time that major Chinese cities, such as Beijing and Shanghai, came within range of India's nuclear weapons. In addition, India's goal of deploying SSBNs equipped with two thousand–kilometer range SLBMs appears to be motivated more by competition with China than Pakistan. China may begin to view India as more of an adversary if China perceives closer security cooperation between India and the United States on sensitive issues such as nuclear energy and missile defense as intended to balance against China. If China begins to reciprocate India's one-sided rivalry with China, the nuclear dynamics in South Asia will become even more unstable.

Even absent a change in Chinese threat perception, changes in China's nuclear force posture aimed at maintaining an assured retaliation capability against the United States could trigger a reaction by India and therefore Pakistan. Chinese development of missile defenses and antisatellite weapons has fueled Indian interest in these technologies. If China views U.S. national missile defense plans as threatening its deterrent, it could respond by deploying MIRVs on the DF-41 ICBM under development. Such a move would increase India's incentive to deploy MIRVs on its own missiles, which would likely provoke a Pakistani reaction, which would further fuel the arms race on the subcontinent. To the extent that India orients its nuclear posture toward China it will face a paradox that "what is credible toward China will likely not be minimum toward Pakistan; and what is minimum toward Pakistan cannot be credible toward China."[78] As a result, this trilateral deterrent relationship among India, Pakistan, and China is inherently unstable.

Conclusion and Policy Recommendations

Strengthening strategic stability faces significant challenges in coping with the more complex geometry of deterrence of the second nuclear age. The new nuclear order is multidimensional on several levels. The bipolar nuclear order of the Cold War has given way to a multipolar nuclear system. Since most nuclear weapon states perceive potential nuclear threats from multiple actors, the deployment of new capabilities or changes in nuclear doctrine by one state can have a ripple effect throughout the system. Recognizing the centrality of the security trilemma—that attempts to deter one state may inadvertently threaten another state—to the second nuclear age is an important step for devising strategies to strengthen strategic stability.

Furthermore, strategic stability is no longer just a product of the interaction between comparable nuclear forces, but increasingly between nuclear forces and nonnuclear technologies such as missile defenses, antisatellite weapons, conventional precision strike weapons, and cyber weapons. These "cross-domain" linkages create new conceptual challenges since the dissimilar properties of these weapons give them different levels of utility for deterrence, war-fighting, coercion, and assurance. The potential for rapid advances in these technologies, at least compared to more mature technologies such as ballistic missiles and nuclear warheads, will make it more difficult for states to accurately assess others' capabilities, which may foster worst-case analyses and arms racing. To the extent that these nonnuclear technologies are developed within different organizations for different purposes, governments will also face bureaucratic hurdles in assessing their cumulative effects on strategic stability.

Strengthening strategic stability will not prevent all crises between nuclear-armed states or guarantee that a future crisis will not escalate into a military dispute or even a nuclear conflict. There is even the

perverse risk that the perception of strategic stability between two
nuclear states will lull decision-makers into a false sense of security and
that they might take unnecessary risks during a crisis based on the belief
that the other side would not dare escalate. Failure to address the loom-
ing challenges to strategic stability, however, presents a greater danger.
Crises can emerge unexpectedly as shown by the terrorist attacks in
Mumbai in 2008, China's unilateral declaration of an air defense identi-
fication zone (ADIZ) in the East China Sea in 2013, and Russia's intervention into Ukraine in 2014. The downing of a Malaysian airplane by a
surface-to-air missile fired from Russian-backed, separatist-controlled
territory in eastern Ukraine in July 2014 vividly demonstrates how such
crises can escalate in unanticipated ways. One can only imagine how the
crisis could have spiraled out of control if the airliner had been American instead of Malaysian.

The United States should proactively shape the second nuclear age
before it finds itself trapped in a new nuclear order that is less stable, less
predictable, and less susceptible to American influence. This approach
will require a long-term effort that will be vulnerable to disruptions by
domestic or international events unrelated to strategic stability. During
the Cold War, the Soviet invasion of Afghanistan derailed U.S. Senate
consent of the Strategic Arms Limitation Talks (SALT) II Treaty. In
South Asia, the incursion of Pakistani forces across the line of control
in Kargil in 1999 wrecked the confidence-building process ushered in
by the Lahore Declaration signed by Pakistani Prime Minister Nawaz
Sharif and Indian Prime Minister Atal Vajpayee. Leaders in all countries need to resist the temptation to sacrifice efforts to strengthen
strategic stability to more immediate but less important exigencies lest
they end up taking steps that are politically popular in the short run but
create greater dangers in the long run.

Strengthening strategic stability should not be seen as a replacement for bilateral strategic arms reductions between the United
States and Russia or as an alternative to nuclear disarmament. The
prospects for renewed U.S.-Russian strategic arms reductions in
the near term, however, are bleak. Even before the crisis in Ukraine
chilled U.S.-Russian relations and the United States charged Russia
with violating the Intermediate-Range Nuclear Forces (INF) Treaty,
significant differences between Washington and Moscow on missile defense, nonstrategic (tactical) nuclear weapons, and long-range

conventional precision strike systems presented significant obstacles to further strategic arms reductions. Nonetheless, strategic, political, and economic incentives will likely lead to a renewed interest in bilateral strategic arms reductions by 2021 when New START is set to expire. Washington and Moscow should not prematurely close this window of opportunity for further strategic arms reductions due to domestic politics or disputes over other foreign policy issues. Likewise, a multilateral treaty to reduce worldwide nuclear arsenals is far over the horizon. Fundamental changes in geopolitics and international relations will need to occur for the nuclear weapon states to view deep reductions as both feasible and desirable. In both cases, the agenda outlined below for mitigating the most serious challenges to strategic stability will help ensure that when the conditions are right for bilateral or multilateral negotiations on nuclear arms reductions, the process will face fewer and lower obstacles.

The following recommendations provide a framework for strengthening strategic stability among the nuclear weapon states through transparency, confidence-building, and dialogue.

MISSILE DEFENSE

The United States should craft a missile defense architecture and policy that provides an effective defense against regional powers such as North Korea and Iran while not threatening the strategic nuclear forces of major powers such as Russia and China. To the extent that concerns over missile defense drive a Russian decision not to further reduce its strategic nuclear arsenal and/or accelerate a Chinese buildup, the United States will have to confront a stark choice between the regional deterrence benefits and the strategic arms control costs of missile defense. It is possible that no national missile defense system is politically acceptable to the United States and is not viewed as threatening in Moscow and Beijing. Nonetheless, the United States will reap diplomatic benefits among its allies in Europe and Asia by continuing its efforts to reassure Russia and China. Being proactive also places the onus on Russia and China to explain how their assessment of the threat posed by Iranian and North Korean missiles differs from that of the United States.

- The Obama administration should continue its efforts, bilaterally and through the NATO-Russia Council, to collaborate with Russia on missile defense, including joint ballistic missile threat assessments, exchange of early warning data, exercises, and computer modeling and simulations.

- The Obama administration should present China with a package of proposals designed to reassure it that the capability and intent of the U.S. national missile defense system is to defend against a limited number of missiles launched by North Korea and Iran. Among these proposals should be explicit public and private reassurances that the United States is not seeking to escape from the current situation of mutual vulnerability with China, reciprocal visits to missile defense test sites, dispatch of observers to missile defense tests and exercises, and joint technical assessments of the North Korean and Iranian missile threats (all of which the United States has already done or has offered to do with Russia).[79]

- The Obama administration should focus on improving the reliability of its existing midcourse interceptors and its ability to discriminate between warheads and decoys before deploying more interceptors at additional locations.[80]

- The Obama administration should discourage India from pursuing missile defense capabilities because these efforts will provoke qualitative and quantitative improvements in Pakistani and Chinese missiles that will circumvent or overwhelm Indian defenses.

ANTISATELLITE WEAPONS

Outer space is a global commons of increasing economic, scientific, and strategic importance. To make space less "congested, competitive, and contested," the United States should pursue the following initiatives with the ultimate goal of dissuading states from testing and deploying ASAT weapons:

- Pursue the multilateral negotiation of a code of conduct in outer space that would maximize the peaceful benefits of space, minimize the risk that military activities will decrease these benefits, and increase the responsibility of all satellite-launching and owning states for maintaining this global resource.

- Seek the cooperation of other satellite-launching nations to develop an international space surveillance network to detect and track space debris, warn satellite operators of potential dangers, and conduct research on ways to reduce the risks that space debris pose to orbiting satellites.[81]

- Negotiate an international agreement that bans activities in space that intentionally generate debris, such as tests of kinetic ASAT weapons. One of the criticisms of a treaty banning ASAT weapons is that it is not verifiable. Verifying compliance with a "no-debris" treaty, however, would be much easier since it is relatively easy to detect events that generate large amounts of space debris.[82]

CONVENTIONAL COUNTERFORCE

- The Obama administration should conduct a thorough interagency review of the potential roles and missions of conventional global prompt strike systems. The review should begin with an assessment of the military value of conventional global prompt strike weapons compared to the current and projected power projection capabilities of the United States' fleet of manned aircraft, cruise missiles, and unmanned aerial vehicles. The review should also consider what impact these types of weapons might have on deterrence, crisis stability, nuclear arms control, and the missile nonproliferation regime as well as the likely reactions of other states.[83] Currently, only the United States and China are conducting tests of hypersonic glider technology, but they may be joined soon by Russia, India, and others. Given the relative immaturity of the technology, the United States has an opportunity to carefully weigh the benefits and risks of this new type of weapon before an arms race develops. If a decision is made to acquire weapons based on hypersonic glider technology, the specific technology selected, its basing mode, and concept of employment should take into account the inherent risks such weapons pose to strategic stability. Therefore, the review should also assess potential measures to mitigate the destabilizing aspects of conventional prompt global strike weapons through the use of confidence-building measures, cooperative monitoring arrangements, and formal arms control agreements.

- The Obama administration should support formalizing information exchanges and notifications among the nuclear weapon states for prelaunch notifications of cruise missile, ballistic missile, and space-launch vehicle (SLV) launches and test flights, including those involving boost-glide and hypersonic glider technologies. The United States and Russia have a bilateral agreement for notification of ballistic missile and SLV launches while India and Pakistan have a similar agreement that covers only ballistic missiles. In addition, the United States, Russia, United Kingdom, and France have signed the Hague Code of Conduct against Ballistic Missile Proliferation, which commits them on a voluntary basis to provide notifications of ballistic missile and SLV launches. There is no uniform prelaunch notification agreement encompassing all nuclear weapon states, however, and no such agreement that covers cruise missiles. In addition to reducing false alarms, a prelaunch notification agreement could serve as a confidence-building measure related to strategic conventional weapons. Notifying other states of tests and operational launches of these types of missiles would minimize the risk that such a launch could be misinterpreted as an attack.[84]

CYBERSECURITY

- The Obama administration should initiate discussions with the other nuclear-armed states on how to improve the cybersecurity of nuclear forces, command and control, and early warning systems. The United States and Russia have already started this process by designating their nuclear risk reduction centers as the channel of communication about cyber incidents that raise national security concerns, and establishing a working group to discuss additional measures to increase cooperation on cybersecurity issues.[85]

- In the interest of avoiding false alarms, unnecessary pressure to launch weapons preemptively during a crisis, or acts that might increase the risk of nuclear weapons being used inadvertently, the United States should initiate a discussion with the other nuclear weapon states on an agreement not to target each other's nuclear forces, including command and control and early warning systems, with cyber weapons.[86] Such an agreement faces several challenges, such as the use of certain command and control systems to conduct both conventional and nuclear operations, the difficulty of verifying compliance, and the even more difficult task of attributing responsibility for violations that are detected. Nonetheless, such a confidence-building measure would establish a "red line" of unacceptable behavior in cyberspace and provide a mechanism for consultation to resolve compliance concerns.

BRIDGING THE GAP AMONG CHINA, INDIA, AND PAKISTAN

The United States conducts regular bilateral strategic dialogues with the other nuclear weapon states, but several of these states do not participate in regular, high-level discussions of nuclear and other strategic issues with each other. This type of dialogue is important for reducing suspicion and misunderstandings, forcing leaders and bureaucrats to spend time and energy on these issues, and a prerequisite for further steps aimed at reassurance and restraint.

- The Obama administration should encourage official government-to-government talks between India and China on issues related to strategic stability, as well as Track 2 dialogues among current and retired government officials and nongovernmental experts. As Lora Saalman has observed, Indian and Chinese nuclear policies and practices overlap considerably, which provides a strong basis for these nations to hold a high-level strategic dialogue on issues such as no first use, minimum deterrence, disarmament, negative security assurances, command and control, nuclear security, ballistic missile defense, antisatellite technology, and civil nuclear energy.[87]

- The United States should encourage India and Pakistan to build on the historic 1999 Lahore Declaration and Memorandum of Understanding and adopt further confidence-building measures to reduce nuclear risks on the subcontinent. Given the politically sensitive nature of high-level talks between India and Pakistan, the Obama administration should recognize that it has little influence over the timing and outcome of such talks. Nonetheless, the United States can build on its past success in cooperating with Chinese policymakers and experts on nuclear issues to make two useful contributions to the success of Indo-Pakistani talks if and when they occur.

- The United States should increase its support for Track 2 diplomatic initiatives between India and Pakistan such as the Ottawa Dialogue.[88] Track 2 dialogues can generate new ideas, provide avenues for information-sharing between nongovernmental experts and policymakers, provide a back channel for government-to-government communication, and build collaborative relations between experts from both sides. China's willingness to lead an effort by the P5 to create a nuclear glossary that provides mutually agreed-upon definitions for important arms control terms demonstrates the positive role that Track 2 efforts can play in stimulating government initiatives. China's willingness to take the lead on this initiative is likely due to its experience with a similar Track 2 exercise between U.S. and Chinese scientists that produced English and Chinese definitions of one thousand terms related to nuclear security.[89]

- The Obama administration should strengthen its support for U.S. government and private initiatives to train and educate promising young scholars, scientists, and practitioners from India and Pakistan in arms control and nonproliferation. The covert nature of the Indian and Pakistani nuclear weapon programs through the late 1990s discouraged public discussions, academic analyses, and even internal debates about nuclear strategy and institutions. When Pakistani and Indian political and military leaders began grappling with the intricacies of nuclear strategy after their 1998 tests, they found their intellectual capital and institutional capacity lacking.[90] The "thinness" of the military and civilian arms control bureaucracies and insufficient depth of expertise outside of government hinders policy formulation, implementation, and evaluation.[91] Increasing the number and depth of interactions among American, Indian, and Pakistani experts from inside and outside of the government who work on issues related to strategic stability can also help dispel myths and misperceptions on all sides. China found itself in a similar situation in the early 1980s as the country began expanding its arms control and nonproliferation commitments. Its government officials, scientists, and academics were able to gain experience with these issues through education and fellowships in the United States and interaction with American colleagues. These activities not only created a cadre of experts who could work inside the bureaucracy, but also socialized them to China's role and responsibilities in the global nonproliferation regime.[92]

MULTIPLE MULTILATERAL APPROACHES NEEDED

Since strategic stability in the second nuclear age is multidimensional, the United States should pursue multiple approaches to working with the other nuclear weapon states to achieve the objectives described above. The United States should pursue a two-pronged approach, building on the success of the P5 nuclear dialogue among the five nuclear weapon states recognized by the NPT and creating a separate forum to include India and Pakistan in discussions on strategic stability.

- The Obama administration should support extending the P5 nuclear dialogue on nuclear arms control and disarmament for another five years and broaden the scope of topics it addresses. The P5 began meeting annually starting in 2009 to discuss transparency, confidence-building, and verification measures.[93] The next phase of this process should move beyond information-sharing sessions about past experiences to knowledge-sharing and more collaborative endeavors to prepare for the future.

- The Obama administration should support greater collaboration among experts from the P5 on the research and development of verification technologies. Each of the P5 already conducts its own research on such technologies but collaboration among them is limited. The initial focus of this collaboration should be on enabling technologies, such as information barriers, radiation detectors, and tamper-proof tags and seals, which would be useful for a wide range of verification tasks.[94] Joint verification exercises designed to demonstrate current capabilities, evaluate emerging technologies, or identify future needs would also be useful.

- The Obama administration should seek multilateral participation in bilateral arms control agreements it has already negotiated with Russia. For example, the United States could invite British, French, and Chinese participants to be observers at practice inspections held by the United States to implement New START.[95] Observers from these nations could also be invited to conduct "ride alongs" for monitoring visits conducted under the auspices of the U.S.-Russian Plutonium Production Reactor Agreement (PPRA), which is designed to confirm the status of shutdown reactors. The inclusion of British,

French, and Chinese participants as observers to any of these processes would demystify the treaty implementation process, provide
firsthand experience with treaty verification, and demonstrate how
managed-access procedures work to provide transparency without
compromising security. The professional conduct of the inspec-
tors and hosts may also help belie the belief that arms control is only
appropriate for adversaries.

- The Obama administration should invite experts from the seven
  established nuclear weapon states to participate in a Strategic Stability Working Group that would discuss measures that could be taken
  individually, collectively, or on a reciprocal basis to reduce the risks
  of nuclear weapons being used deliberately, by accident, or in an
  unauthorized manner. The P5 nuclear dialogue, which was formed
  in relation to the NPT, cannot be expanded to include India and Pakistan, since neither country has signed the treaty. Though India and
  Pakistan already participate in the "P5 plus" talks in Geneva, these
  talks are typically conducted by diplomats and focused primarily on issues related to negotiations on the Fissile Material Cutoff
  Treaty (FMCT).[96] The Strategic Stability Working Group would
  have a broader scope and include a wider range of government officials capable of addressing current and potential challenges to strategic stability. Although nonnuclear weapon states might argue that
  inviting India and Pakistan to participate in this forum rewards them
  for remaining outside the nonproliferation regime, the stakes are
  too high to allow principles to overwhelm pragmatism. India and
  Pakistan have growing stockpiles of fissile material and arsenals of
  nuclear weapons, and are at high risk of another conflict. In addition, their competition threatens progress on other nonproliferation
  issues such as FMCT, the Comprehensive Test Ban Treaty (CTBT),
  and the security of nuclear materials. Creating a venue for the seven
  established nuclear weapon states to discuss issues related to strategic
  stability has several advantages. The interaction among China, India,
  and Pakistan, the only nuclear states increasing their nuclear arsenals,
  will have a strong influence on strategic stability in the years ahead.
  This approach avoids the charges of discrimination that have dogged
  previous arms control and nonproliferation initiatives in South Asia.
  In addition, a broader forum might provide political cover to jump-
  start a Sino-Indian nuclear dialogue, shelter an Indo-Pakistani dialogue from the vagaries of their domestic politics and international

crises, and provide an opportunity for the United States and Pakistan to continue discussing these issues at times when their bilateral relations are poor. Finally, this working group could provide another mechanism for multilateralizing previously agreed-to or future bilateral agreements. This group might be the proper forum to negotiate the prelaunch notification agreement described above. Another opportunity to broaden the scope of a bilateral agreement may arise if the next round of U.S.-Russian strategic arms control manages to eliminate land-based MIRVed missiles (which currently only Russia possesses). The members of the group could collectively pledge not to deploy such weapons, forestalling an arms race between China and India in this technology. Indeed, knowing that China would commit not to deploy MIRVs might make it easier for Russia to agree to eliminate its own MIRVs.

The concept of strategic stability originated during the Cold War as a way of understanding what factors might make the use of nuclear weapons more or less likely. As long as nuclear weapons exist, it is in the U.S. national interest to reduce the likelihood that these weapons will be used—whether on purpose, inadvertently, or without authorization. The transition from the first nuclear age to the second age has introduced new nuclear powers, new sources of uncertainty, and a new geometry of deterrence. Though the nuclear weapon states have come a long way in replacing the balance of terror with prudence, maintaining this balance still requires "eternal vigilance and skill."[97] Former Senator Sam Nunn has likened reducing the dangers posed by nuclear weapons to climbing a mountain.[98] The policies adopted by the Obama administration before the end of its term will help determine how many paths are available to future policymakers and how steep their climb will be.

Endnotes

1. Colin S. Gray, *The Second Nuclear Age* (Boulder, CO: Lynne Reinner, 1999); Paul Bracken, *The Second Nuclear Age: Strategy, Danger, and the New Power Politics* (New York: Times Books, 2012).
2. Linton Brooks and Mira Rapp-Hooper, "Extended Deterrence, Assurance, and Reassurance in the Pacific during the Second Nuclear Age," in Ashley J. Tellis, Abraham M. Denmark, and Travis Tanner, eds., *Strategic Asia 2013-14: Asia in the Second Nuclear Age* (Washington, DC: National Bureau of Asia Research, 2013), pp. 292–93.
3. The grouping of these seven states together is for analytical purposes and is not related to the legality of their possession of nuclear weapons under the 1968 Nuclear Nonproliferation Treaty (NPT).
4. Hans M. Kristensen and Robert S. Norris, "Global Nuclear Weapons Inventories, 1945-2013," *Bulletin of the Atomic Scientists* 69, no. 5, September/October 2013, pp. 75–81.
5. International Institute for Strategic Studies, *The Military Balance 2014* (Oxford: Routledge, 2014), p. 254.
6. Paolo Foradori and Martin B. Malin, eds., "A WMD–Free Zone in the Middle East: Regional Perspectives," Belfer Center for Science and International Affairs, November 2013; and John S. Park, "Inside Multilateralism: The Six-Party Talks," *Washington Quarterly* 28, no. 4, Autumn 2005, pp. 75–91.
7. Department of State, "Fact Sheet: Transparency in the U.S. Nuclear Weapons Stockpile," April 28, 2014; Hans M. Kristensen and Robert S. Norris, "US Nuclear Forces, 2014," *Bulletin of the Atomic Scientists* 70, no. 1, January/February 2014, pp. 85–93.
8. Hans M. Kristensen and Robert S. Norris, "Russian Nuclear Forces, 2014," *Bulletin of the Atomic Scientists* 70, no. 2, March/April 2014, p. 77.
9. These countries include the twenty-seven other members of the North Atlantic Treaty Organization (NATO), as well as Australia, Japan, and South Korea. The United States has signed mutual defense treaties with additional states and designated even more countries as "major non-NATO allies" for the purpose of enhancing security cooperation, but is not believed to have provided any of them with formal assurances that nuclear weapons would be used to guarantee their security.
10. Department of Defense, "Nuclear Posture Review," April 2010.
11. Russian Federation, "The Military Doctrine of the Russian Federation," February 5, 2010, pp. 8–9.
12. Nikolai Sokov, "Assessing Russian Attitudes Toward Phased, Deep Nuclear Reductions," *Nonproliferation Review* 20, no. 2, July 2013, pp. 252–53; and Dmitri Trenin, "Russian Perspectives on the Global Elimination of Nuclear Weapons," in Barry Blechman, ed., *Russia and the United States: Unblocking the Road to Zero* (Washington, DC: Henry L. Stimson Center, 2009), pp. 4–5.
13. Frank Klotz, "The Future of Britain's Nuclear Deterrent," *National Interest*, July 24, 2013, http://nationalinterest.org/commentary/the-future-britains-nuclear-deterrent-8768

14. Republic of France, "Reporting by France on Actions 5, 20 and 21 of the 2010 NPT Review Conference Final Document," May 2014, p. 4.
15. The United Kingdom of Great Britain and Northern Ireland, "National Report Pursuant to Actions 5, 20, and 21 of the NPT Review Conference Final Document," May 2014, p. 2; Republic of France, "Reporting by France on Actions 5, 20 and 21 of the 2010 NPT Review Conference Final Document," p. 4.
16. Cabinet Office, "Securing Britain in an Age of Uncertainty: The Strategic Defence and Security Review," October 2010, p. 37.
17. Republic of France, "French White Paper on Defence and National Security," 2013, p. 67.
18. Information Office of the State Council of the People's Republic of China, "China's National Defense in 2006," http://eng.mod.gov.cn/Database/WhitePapers/2006.htm.
19. M. Taylor Fravel and Evan S. Medeiros, "China's Search for Assured Retaliation: The Evolution of Chinese Nuclear Strategy and Force Structure," *International Security* 35, no. 2, Fall 2010, pp. 48–87.
20. Christopher P. Twomey, "Nuclear Stability at Low Numbers: The Perspective from Beijing," *Nonproliferation Review* 20, no. 2, July 2013, pp. 289–303.
21. Hans M. Kristensen and Robert S. Norris, "Chinese Nuclear Forces, 2013," *Bulletin of the Atomic Scientists* 69, no. 6, November/December 2014, pp. 80–82.
22. Mark Fitzpatrick, *Overcoming Pakistan's Nuclear Dangers*, Adelphi Series No. 443 (London: International Institute for Strategic Studies, 2013), pp. 18–22.
23. Christopher Clary, "The Future of Pakistan's Nuclear Weapons Program," in Ashley J. Tellis, Abraham M. Denmark, and Travis Tanner, eds., *Strategic Asia 2013-14: Asia in the Second Nuclear Age* (Washington, DC: National Bureau of Asia Research, 2013), pp. 135–37.
24. Fitzpatrick, *Overcoming Pakistan's Nuclear Dangers*, pp. 24–26.
25. Peter R. Lavoy, "Islamabad's Nuclear Posture: Its Premises and Implementation," in Henry Sokolski, ed., *Pakistan's Nuclear Future: Worries Beyond War* (Carlisle Barracks, PA: Strategic Studies Institute, 2008), pp. 129–65.
26. Clary, "The Future of Pakistan's Nuclear Weapons Program," pp. 141–42.
27. Fitzpatrick, *Overcoming Pakistan's Nuclear Dangers*, pp. 124–25.
28. Vipin Narang, "Five Myths About India's Nuclear Posture," *Washington Quarterly* 36, no. 3, Summer 2013, pp. 148–49.
29. Prime Minister's Office, "Cabinet Committee on Security Reviews Progress in Operationalizing India's Nuclear Doctrine," January 4, 2003.
30. P. R. Chari, "India's Nuclear Doctrine: Stirrings of Change," *Carnegie Endowment for International Peace*, June 4, 2014, http://carnegieendowment.org/2014/06/04/india-s-nuclear-doctrine-stirrings-of-change/hcks.
31. Elbridge A. Colby and Michael S. Gerson, eds., *Strategic Stability: Contending Interpretations* (Carlisle Barracks, PA: Strategic Studies Institute, 2013).
32. Thomas C. Schelling and Morton H. Halperin, *Strategy and Arms Control* (New York: Twentieth Century Fund, 1961), p. 50.
33. Brooks and Rapp-Hooper, "Extended Deterrence, Assurance, and Reassurance in the Pacific during the Second Nuclear Age," pp. 292–93.
34. The size of the circles and the degree of overlap between them are not to scale and are not meant to indicate any qualitative or quantitative information about the relationships depicted in the figure.
35. Harsh V. Pant, "The Pakistan Thorn in China-India-U.S. Relations," *The Washington Quarterly* 35, no. 1, Winter 2012, pp. 83–95.
36. Anne Gearan, "U.S. Beefs Up West Coast Missile Defenses in Face of N. Korea Threat," *Washington Post*, March 15, 2013.

37. Remarks by Frank A. Rose, deputy assistant secretary of state, Bureau of Arms Control, verification and compliance, to the Missile Defense Conference, Royal United Services Institute (RUSI), London, June 12, 2013, http://www.state.gov/t/avc/rls/2013/210565.htm.
38. Ian E. Rinehart, Steven A. Hildreth, and Susan V. Lawrence, "Ballistic Missile Defense in the Asia-Pacific Region: Cooperation and Opposition," Congressional Research Service, June 24, 2013.
39. Department of Defense, "Ballistic Missile Defense Review Report," February 2010, pp. 4–7, 12–13.
40. Wu Riqiang, "China's Anxiety About US Missile Defence: A Solution," *Survival* 55, no. 5, October/November 2013, pp. 29–52.
41. Gregory D. Koblentz, "Theater Missile Defense and South Asia: A Volatile Mix," *Nonproliferation Review* 3, no. 4, Spring/Summer 1997, pp. 54–62.
42. Feroz Hassan Khan, *Eating Grass: The Making of the Pakistani Bomb* (Stanford, CA: Stanford University Press, 2012), pp. 387–88; and Dennis M. Gormley, *Missile Contagion: Cruise Missile Proliferation and the Threat to International Security* (Annapolis, MD: Naval Institute Press, 2008), pp. 69–74.
43. Ting Shi, "China Says Third Missile-Defense Test in Four Years Successful," *Bloomberg*, July 24, 2014.
44. Timothy Farnsworth, "China Conducts Missile Defense Test," *Arms Control Today*, March 2013; Department of Defense, "Military and Security Developments Involving the People's Republic of China 2014," 2014, p. 34.
45. Rajeswari Pillai Rajagopalan, "Linking Strategic Stability and Ballistic Missile Defense: The View From India," in Lora Saalman, ed. and trans., *The China-India Nuclear Crossroads* (Washington, DC: Carnegie Endowment for International Peace, 2012), pp. 65–69.
46. Kurt Gottfried and Richard Ned Lebow, "Anti-Satellite Weapons: Weighing the Risks," *Daedalus* 114, no. 2, Spring 1985, pp. 147–69; Matthew Mowthorpe, *The Militarization and Weaponization of Space* (New York: Lexington Books, 2004), p. 110.
47. Mark A. Stokes with Dean Cheng, "China's Evolving Space Capabilities: Implications for U.S. Interests," Project 2049 Institute, April 26, 2012; "China Seen Readying Space-Based Warning Sensor," *Global Security Newswire*, July 25, 2013.
48. Brian Weeden, "Through a Glass, Darkly: Chinese, American, and Russian Anti-Satellite Testing in Space," Secure World Foundation, March 2014.
49. Jana Honkova, "The Russian Federation's Approach to Military Space and Its Military Space Capabilities," George C. Marshall Institute, November 2013.
50. "Navy Missile Hits Dying Spy Satellite, Says Pentagon," CNN, February 21, 2008.
51. Brian Weeden, "Anti-satellite Tests in Space: The Case of China," Secure World Foundation, August 16, 2013; Marcia Smith, "U.S. Accuses China of Conducting Another ASAT Test," *Space Policy Online*, July 25, 2014, http://www.spacepolicyonline.com/news/u-s-accuses-china-of-conducting-another-asat-test.
52. Rajeswari Pillai Rajagoapalan, "India's Changing Policy on Space Militarization: The Impact of China's ASAT Test," *India Review* 10, no. 4, October–December 2011, pp. 354–78.
53. James M. Acton, "Silver Bullet? Asking the Right Questions About Conventional Prompt Global Strike," Carnegie Endowment for International Peace, 2013.
54. Dennis M. Gormley, "Sixty Minutes to Strike: Assessing the Risks, Benefits, and Arms Control Implications of Conventional Prompt Global Strike," *Sicherheit und Frieden* (Security and Peace) 1, 2014, pp. 36–46.
55. For a similar list, see Acton, "Silver Bullet?" pp. 111–29.
56. National Research Council, *Conventional Prompt Global Strike: Issues for 2008 and Beyond* (Washington, DC: National Academies Press, 2008), p. 192.

57. Gormley, "Sixty Minutes to Strike," pp. 36–46.
58. Acton, "Silver Bullet?" pp. 97–107.
59. Eugene Miasnikov, "Strategic Conventional Weapons and Stability," presentation at the workshop on strategic stability and arms control, Carnegie-Tsinghua Center for Global Policy, Beijing, China, April 23–24, 2012, http://www.armscontrol.ru/pubs/en/emo42312.html; Tong Zhao, "Conventional Counterforce Strike: An Option for Damage Limitation in Conflicts with Nuclear-Armed Adversaries?" *Science and Global Security* 19, no. 3, 2011, pp. 195–222.
60. John D. Steinbruner, "Nuclear Decapitation," *Foreign Policy* 45, Winter 1981–1982, pp. 16–28.
61. William Owens, Kenneth W. Dam, and Herbert S. Lin, eds., *Technology, Policy, Law, and Ethics Regarding U.S. Acquisition and Use of Cyberattack Capabilities* (Washington, DC: National Academies Press, 2009), p. 296.
62. Defense Science Board, "Resilient Military Systems and the Advanced Cyber Threat," Department of Defense, January 2013, p. 7; Senate Armed Services Committee, *Hearing to Receive Testimony on U.S. Strategic Command and U.S. Cyber Command in Review of the Defense Authorization Request for Fiscal Year 2014 and the Future Years Defense Program* (Washington, DC: U.S. Government Printing Office, 2013), p. 10.
63. Lesley Stahl, "Who's Minding the Nukes?" *60 Minutes*, April 27, 2014, http://www.cbsnews.com/news/whos-minding-the-nuclear-weapons/.
64. Scott D. Sagan, *The Limits of Safety: Organizations, Accidents, and Nuclear Weapons* (Princeton, NJ: Princeton University Press, 1993), pp. 225–46; William Burr, "The 3 A.M. Phone Call: False Warnings of Soviet Missile Attacks During 1979–80 Led to Alert Actions for U.S. Strategic Forces," National Security Archive Electronic Briefing Book No. 371, National Security Archive, March 1, 2012, http://www2.gwu.edu/~nsarchiv/nukevault/ebb371/#_ednref9.
65. David A. Fulghum and Robert Wall, "Cyber-Combat's First Shot," *Aviation Week & Space Technology*, November 26, 2007; Richard A. Clarke and Robert K. Kake, *Cyber War: The Next Threat to National Security and What to Do About It* (New York: HarperCollins, 2010), pp. 6–8.
66. "Air Force Loses Contact With 50 ICBMs at Wyoming Base," *Global Security Newswire*, October 27, 2010,
67. Schelling and Halperin, *Strategy and Arms Control*, p. 33.
68. Owens, Dam, and Lin, *Technology, Policy, Law, and Ethics Regarding U.S. Acquisition and Use of Cyberattack Capabilities*, pp. 296–97.
69. Bruce G. Blair, *The Logic of Accidental Nuclear War* (Washington, DC: Brookings Institution Press, 1993); David E. Hoffman, *The Dead Hand: The Untold Story of the Cold War Arms Race and Its Dangerous Legacy* (New York: Doubleday, 2009).
70. Shasank Joshi, "Pakistan's Tactical Nuclear Nightmare: Déja Vu?" *The Washington Quarterly* 36, no. 3, Summer 2013, pp. 159–72; Clary, "The Future of Pakistan's Nuclear Weapons Program," pp. 131–60.
71. On the growing conventional military imbalance between India and Pakistan, see John H. Gill, "India and Pakistan: A Shift in the Military Calculus?" in Ashley J. Tellis and Michael Wills, eds., *Strategic Asia 2005–06: Military Modernization in an Era of Uncertainty* (Washington, DC: National Bureau of Asia Research, 2005), pp. 263–65; and Usman Ansari, "Pakistan Again Boosts Defense Budget, But at Smaller Rate," *Defense News*, June 5, 2014.
72. Scott D. Sagan, "Introduction," in Scott D. Sagan, ed., *Inside Nuclear South Asia* (Stanford, CA: Stanford University Press, 2009), p. 16.
73. Christopher Clary, "Thinking About Pakistan's Nuclear Security in Peacetime, Crisis and War," Institute for Defence Studies and Analyses, 2010.

74. Narang, "Five Myths About India's Nuclear Posture," pp. 148–49; Joshi, "Pakistan's Tactical Nuclear Nightmare," pp. 165–166.

75. Lora Saalman, ed. and trans., *The China-India Nuclear Crossroads* (Washington, DC: Carnegie Endowment for International Peace, 2012).

76. Guarav Kampani, "India: The Challenges of Nuclear Operationalization and Strategic Stability," in Tellis, Denmark, and Tanner, eds., *Strategic Asia 2013-14*, pp. 103–04.

77. Eben Lindsey, Michael Glosny, and Christopher Twomey, "US-China Strategic Dialogue, Phase VI: An NPS and Pacific Forum Conference," Naval Postgraduate School, November 2011, p. 10.

78. Narang, "Five Myths about India's Nuclear Posture," p. 144.

79. Elbridge A. Colby and Abraham M. Denmark, "Nuclear Weapons and U.S.-China Relations: A Way Forward," Center for Strategic and International Studies, March 2013.

80. National Research Council, *Making Sense of Ballistic Missile Defense: An Assessment of Concepts and Systems for U.S. Boost-Phase Missile Defense in Comparison to Other Alternatives* (Washington, DC: National Academies Press, 2012).

81. For a longer list of similar recommendations, see Micah Zenko, "Dangerous Space Incidents," Council on Foreign Relations, April 2014, pp. 5–8.

82. Ross Liemer and Christopher F. Chyba, "A Verifiable Limited Test Ban for Anti-Satellite Weapons," *Washington Quarterly* 33, no. 3, July 2010, pp. 149–63.

83. James M. Acton, "Silver Bullet."

84. M. Elaine Bunn and Vincent A. Manzo, "Conventional Prompt Global Strike: Strategic Asset or Unusable Liability?" *Strategic Forum* no. 263, National Defense University, February 2011.

85. Ellen Nakashima, "U.S. and Russia Sign Pact to Create Communication Link on Cyber Security," *Washington Post*, June 17, 2013.

86. For a similar proposal, see Richard J. Danzig, "Surviving on a Diet of Poisoned Fruit: Reducing the National Security Risks of America's Cyber Dependencies," Center for New American Security, July 2014, pp. 24–27.

87. Lora Saalman, "Conclusion: Comparing the Comparable," in *The China-India Nuclear Crossroads*, pp. 183–84.

88. The Ottawa Dialogue, http://socialsciences.uottawa.ca/dialogue/eng/.

89. National Academy of Sciences and Chinese People's Association for Peace and Disarmament, *English-Chinese, Chinese-English Nuclear Security Glossary* (Washington, DC: National Academies Press and Beijing: Atomic Energy Press, 2008).

90. Khan, *Eating Grass*, pp. 321–37; Verghese Koithara, *Managing India's Nuclear Forces* (Washington, DC: Brookings Institution Press, 2012), pp. 90–94.

91. Interviews with current and former State Department officials, Washington, DC, June 2014.

92. Evan S. Medeiros, *Reluctant Restraint: The Evolution of China's Nonproliferation Policies and Practices, 1980–2004* (Stanford, CAw: Stanford University Press, 2007); Wendy Frieman, *China, Arms Control, and Nonproliferation* (London: Routledge, 2004).

93. Andrea Berger and Malcolm Chalmers, *Great Expectations: The P5 Process and the Non-Proliferation Treaty*, Whitehall Paper 3-13 (London: RUSI, 2013); Nick Ritchie, *Pathways and Purposes for P-5 Nuclear Dialogue* (London: European Leadership Network, September 2013).

94. Defense Science Board, "Assessment of Nuclear Monitoring and Verification Technologies," Department of Defense, January 2014; and Nuclear Threat Initiative, "Innovating Verification: New Tools and New Actors to Reduce Nuclear Risks—Overview," Nuclear Threat Initiative, 2014, pp. 9–11.

95. Linton F. Brooks, "Looking to the Future: The Post-New Start World and Potential Sino-U.S. Confidence Building Measures," in Eben Lindsey, Michael Glosny, and

Christopher Twomey, "US-China Strategic Dialogue, Phase VI: An NPS and Pacific Forum Conference," Naval Postgraduate School, November 2011, p. 35.

96. Andrea Berger, "Finding the Right Home for FMCT Talks," *Arms Control Today*, October 2012; Interview with Department of State official, June 2010.

97. Schelling and Halperin, *Strategy and Arms Control*, p. 59.

98. Daryl G. Kimball and Miles A. Pomper, "A World Free of Nuclear Weapons: An Interview with Nuclear Threat Initiative Co-Chairman Sam Nunn," *Arms Control Today*, March 2008.

About the Author

Gregory D. Koblentz is an associate professor in the School of Policy, Government, and International Affairs and deputy director of the biodefense graduate program at George Mason University. Koblentz is a research affiliate with the security studies program at the Massachusetts Institute of Technology and a member of the scientist working group on chemical and biological weapons at the Center for Arms Control and Non-Proliferation in Washington, DC. During 2012–2013, he was a Stanton Nuclear Security Fellow at the Council on Foreign Relations. Previously, he worked at Georgetown University, Harvard University's Kennedy School of Government, and the Carnegie Endowment for International Peace.

Koblentz has published in international security journals including *International Security, Survival, Contemporary Security Policy, International Affairs, Bioterrorism and Biosecurity*, and *Nonproliferation Review*. He is the author of *Living Weapons: Biological Warfare and International Security* and coauthor of *Tracking Nuclear Proliferation: A Guide in Maps and Charts*. He received an MPP from the John F. Kennedy School of Government at Harvard University and a PhD from the Massachusetts Institute of Technology.

Advisory Committee for
Strategic Stability in the Second Nuclear Age

This report reflects the judgments and recommendations of the authors. It does not necessarily represent the views of members of the advisory committee, whose involvement in no way should be interpreted as an endorsement of the report by either themselves or the organizations with which they are affiliated.

Amy Woolf
Congressional Research Service

Stephen M. Younger
Northrop Grumman

Micah Zenko, *ex officio*
Council on Foreign Relations

Council Special Reports

Published by the Council on Foreign Relations

UN Security Council Enlargement and U.S. Interests
Kara C. McDonald and Stewart M. Patrick; CSR No. 59, December 2010
An International Institutions and Global Governance Program Report

Congress and National Security
Kay King; CSR No. 58, November 2010

Toward Deeper Reductions in U.S. and Russian Nuclear Weapons
Micah Zenko; CSR No. 57, November 2010
A Center for Preventive Action Report

Internet Governance in an Age of Cyber Insecurity
Robert K. Knake; CSR No. 56, September 2010
An International Institutions and Global Governance Program Report

From Rome to Kampala: The U.S. Approach to the 2010 International Criminal Court Review Conference
Vijay Padmanabhan; CSR No. 55, April 2010

Strengthening the Nuclear Nonproliferation Regime
Paul Lettow; CSR No. 54, April 2010
An International Institutions and Global Governance Program Report

The Russian Economic Crisis
Jeffrey Mankoff; CSR No. 53, April 2010

Somalia: A New Approach
Bronwyn E. Bruton; CSR No. 52, March 2010
A Center for Preventive Action Report

The Future of NATO
James M. Goldgeier; CSR No. 51, February 2010
An International Institutions and Global Governance Program Report

The United States in the New Asia
Evan A. Feigenbaum and Robert A. Manning; CSR No. 50, November 2009
An International Institutions and Global Governance Program Report

Intervention to Stop Genocide and Mass Atrocities: International Norms and U.S. Policy
Matthew C. Waxman; CSR No. 49, October 2009
An International Institutions and Global Governance Program Report

Enhancing U.S. Preventive Action
Paul B. Stares and Micah Zenko; CSR No. 48, October 2009
A Center for Preventive Action Report

The Canadian Oil Sands: Energy Security vs. Climate Change
Michael A. Levi; CSR No. 47, May 2009
A Maurice R. Greenberg Center for Geoeconomic Studies Report

The National Interest and the Law of the Sea
Scott G. Borgerson; CSR No. 46, May 2009

Lessons of the Financial Crisis
Benn Steil; CSR No. 45, March 2009
A Maurice R. Greenberg Center for Geoeconomic Studies Report

Global Imbalances and the Financial Crisis
Steven Dunaway; CSR No. 44, March 2009
A Maurice R. Greenberg Center for Geoeconomic Studies Report

Eurasian Energy Security
Jeffrey Mankoff; CSR No. 43, February 2009

Preparing for Sudden Change in North Korea
Paul B. Stares and Joel S. Wit; CSR No. 42, January 2009
A Center for Preventive Action Report

Averting Crisis in Ukraine
Steven Pifer; CSR No. 41, January 2009
A Center for Preventive Action Report

Congo: Securing Peace, Sustaining Progress
Anthony W. Gambino; CSR No. 40, October 2008
A Center for Preventive Action Report

Deterring State Sponsorship of Nuclear Terrorism
Michael A. Levi; CSR No. 39, September 2008

China, Space Weapons, and U.S. Security
Bruce W. MacDonald; CSR No. 38, September 2008

Sovereign Wealth and Sovereign Power: The Strategic Consequences of American Indebtedness
Brad W. Setser; CSR No. 37, September 2008
A Maurice R. Greenberg Center for Geoeconomic Studies Report

Securing Pakistan's Tribal Belt
Daniel S. Markey; CSR No. 36, July 2008 (web-only release) and August 2008
A Center for Preventive Action Report

Avoiding Transfers to Torture
Ashley S. Deeks; CSR No. 35, June 2008

Global FDI Policy: Correcting a Protectionist Drift
David M. Marchick and Matthew J. Slaughter; CSR No. 34, June 2008
A Maurice R. Greenberg Center for Geoeconomic Studies Report

Dealing with Damascus: Seeking a Greater Return on U.S.-Syria Relations
Mona Yacoubian and Scott Lasensky; CSR No. 33, June 2008
A Center for Preventive Action Report

Climate Change and National Security: An Agenda for Action
Joshua W. Busby; CSR No. 32, November 2007
A Maurice R. Greenberg Center for Geoeconomic Studies Report

Planning for Post-Mugabe Zimbabwe
Michelle D. Gavin; CSR No. 31, October 2007
A Center for Preventive Action Report

The Case for Wage Insurance
Robert J. LaLonde; CSR No. 30, September 2007
A Maurice R. Greenberg Center for Geoeconomic Studies Report

Reform of the International Monetary Fund
Peter B. Kenen; CSR No. 29, May 2007
A Maurice R. Greenberg Center for Geoeconomic Studies Report

Nuclear Energy: Balancing Benefits and Risks
Charles D. Ferguson; CSR No. 28, April 2007

Nigeria: Elections and Continuing Challenges
Robert I. Rotberg; CSR No. 27, April 2007
A Center for Preventive Action Report

The Economic Logic of Illegal Immigration
Gordon H. Hanson; CSR No. 26, April 2007
A Maurice R. Greenberg Center for Geoeconomic Studies Report

The United States and the WTO Dispute Settlement System
Robert Z. Lawrence; CSR No. 25, March 2007
A Maurice R. Greenberg Center for Geoeconomic Studies Report

Bolivia on the Brink
Eduardo A. Gamarra; CSR No. 24, February 2007
A Center for Preventive Action Report

After the Surge: The Case for U.S. Military Disengagement From Iraq
Steven N. Simon; CSR No. 23, February 2007

Darfur and Beyond: What Is Needed to Prevent Mass Atrocities
Lee Feinstein; CSR No. 22, January 2007

Avoiding Conflict in the Horn of Africa: U.S. Policy Toward Ethiopia and Eritrea
Terrence Lyons; CSR No. 21, December 2006
A Center for Preventive Action Report

Living with Hugo: U.S. Policy Toward Hugo Chávez's Venezuela
Richard Lapper; CSR No. 20, November 2006
A Center for Preventive Action Report

Reforming U.S. Patent Policy: Getting the Incentives Right
Keith E. Maskus; CSR No. 19, November 2006
A Maurice R. Greenberg Center for Geoeconomic Studies Report

Foreign Investment and National Security: Getting the Balance Right
Alan P. Larson and David M. Marchick; CSR No. 18, July 2006
A Maurice R. Greenberg Center for Geoeconomic Studies Report

Challenges for a Postelection Mexico: Issues for U.S. Policy
Pamela K. Starr; CSR No. 17, June 2006 (web-only release) and November 2006

U.S.-India Nuclear Cooperation: A Strategy for Moving Forward
Michael A. Levi and Charles D. Ferguson; CSR No. 16, June 2006

Generating Momentum for a New Era in U.S.-Turkey Relations
Steven A. Cook and Elizabeth Sherwood-Randall; CSR No. 15, June 2006

Peace in Papua: Widening a Window of Opportunity
Blair A. King; CSR No. 14, March 2006
A Center for Preventive Action Report

Neglected Defense: Mobilizing the Private Sector to Support Homeland Security
Stephen E. Flynn and Daniel B. Prieto; CSR No. 13, March 2006

Afghanistan's Uncertain Transition From Turmoil to Normalcy
Barnett R. Rubin; CSR No. 12, March 2006
A Center for Preventive Action Report

Preventing Catastrophic Nuclear Terrorism
Charles D. Ferguson; CSR No. 11, March 2006

Getting Serious About the Twin Deficits
Menzie D. Chinn; CSR No. 10, September 2005
A Maurice R. Greenberg Center for Geoeconomic Studies Report

Both Sides of the Aisle: A Call for Bipartisan Foreign Policy
Nancy E. Roman; CSR No. 9, September 2005

Forgotten Intervention? What the United States Needs to Do in the Western Balkans
Amelia Branczik and William L. Nash; CSR No. 8, June 2005
A Center for Preventive Action Report

A New Beginning: Strategies for a More Fruitful Dialogue with the Muslim World
Craig Charney and Nicole Yakatan; CSR No. 7, May 2005

Power-Sharing in Iraq
David L. Phillips; CSR No. 6, April 2005
A Center for Preventive Action Report

Giving Meaning to "Never Again": Seeking an Effective Response to the Crisis in Darfur and Beyond
Cheryl O. Igiri and Princeton N. Lyman; CSR No. 5, September 2004

Freedom, Prosperity, and Security: The G8 Partnership with Africa: Sea Island 2004 and Beyond
J. Brian Atwood, Robert S. Browne, and Princeton N. Lyman; CSR No. 4, May 2004

Addressing the HIV/AIDS Pandemic: A U.S. Global AIDS Strategy for the Long Term
Daniel M. Fox and Princeton N. Lyman; CSR No. 3, May 2004
Cosponsored with the Milbank Memorial Fund

Challenges for a Post-Election Philippines
Catharin E. Dalpino; CSR No. 2, May 2004
A Center for Preventive Action Report

Stability, Security, and Sovereignty in the Republic of Georgia
David L. Phillips; CSR No. 1, January 2004
A Center for Preventive Action Report